Unpopular Culture

Grayson Perry Selects from the Arts Council Collection

ARTS COUNCIL ENGLAND

SOUTHBANK CENTRE **HAYWARD PUBLISHING**

Published on the occasion of the
exhibition *Unpopular Culture:
Grayson Perry Selects from the Arts
Council Collection*, an Arts Council
Collection touring exhibition

Exhibition tour:
De La Warr Pavilion, Bexhill on Sea:
10 May – 6 July 2008
Harris Museum and Art Gallery, Preston:
19 July – 14 September
DLI Museum and Art Gallery, Durham:
15 November 2008 – 4 January 2009
Southampton City Art Gallery,
Southampton: 17 January – 15 March
Aberystwyth Arts Centre, Aberystwyth:
21 March – 10 May
Scarborough Art Gallery, Scarborough:
16 May – 5 July
Longside Gallery, Wakefield:
18 July – 25 October
Victoria Art Gallery, Bath:
7 November – 3 January 2010

Exhibition curated by Grayson Perry

Exhibition organised by Natalie Rudd
and Jill Constantine with assistance from
Lizzie Docherty and Rachel Arndt

Arts Council Collection team:
Christie Coutin, Monika McConnell,
Andy Craig, Sussanah Chan, Alex Flinn,
Richard Morrow, Jonny Aldous, Ann Jones

Art Publisher: Caroline Wetherilt
Publishing Co-ordinator: Giselle Osborne
Sales Manager: Deborah Power
Catalogue designed by Valle Walkley
Printed in Italy by Graphicom

Front cover, p. 6: Photos by Eric Great-Rex

Published by Hayward Publishing,
Southbank Centre, Belvedere Road,
London, SE1 8XX, UK
www.southbankcentre.co.uk
© The Hayward 2008

Texts © the authors 2008
(unless otherwise stated)
p. 23: © The Estate of Vernon Scannell
p. 32: Tony Harrison – Collected Poems
(Penguin 2007)
pp. 39, 65–66, 84: © Faber and Faber Ltd
and the Philip Larkin Estate

Artworks / photographs © the artists 2008
or © estate of the artists 2008
(unless otherwise stated)
Reproductions: Anna Arca,
Jerry Hardman-Jones, Marcus Leith,
Red Head Photography, Jonty Wilde

Distributed in North America, Central
America and South America by D.A.P. /
Distributed Art Publishers, 155 Sixth
Avenue, 2nd Floor, New York, N.Y. 10013,
tel: +212 627 1999, fax: +212 627 9484,
www.artbook.com

Distributed outside North and South
America by Cornerhouse Publications,
70 Oxford Street, Manchester M1 5NH,
tel: +44 (0) 161 200 1503, fax: +44 (0) 161
200 1504, www.cornerhouse.org/books

ARTS COUNCIL COLLECTION AT
SOUTHBANK CENTRE

SOUTHBANK CENTRE HAYWARD TOURING

Preface

'Always the same picture: high summer, the long days in the sun, slim volumes of verse, crisp linen, the smell of starch. What a romantic picture. Phoney too, of course. It must have rained sometimes.'

Jimmy Porter, in John Osborne, *Look Back In Anger*, 1956

WHEN DID THE ENGLISH change from being a literary nation to one so concerned with visual art? For many centuries, ours was one of the least distinguished traditions of visual art in Europe. In his book, *The English*, Jeremy Paxman suggests that the English Reformation was a key factor, having been 'about politics, rationality and choice', and argues that 'therefore words were the medium of choice'. Now, as Grayson Perry notes in his essay here, our major art venues throng with people, and 'celebrity culture' embraces artists to make household names of them. The artists whose artwork is represented in *Unpopular Culture* were making work under very different circumstances, and the selection Grayson Perry has made owes its fascination to the traction between differing political and intellectual positions.

Perry has woven together a complex post-war conversation; one that embraces the romantic nostalgia represented by Duncan Grant's *Cow Stalls* and the landscapes of Robert Colquhoun and Elinor Bellingham Smith, but interjects the anxiety of the new nuclear age in the 1950s, as dramatically expressed by Kenneth Armitage. He sets the sculpture of Barbara Hepworth and Henry Moore, so embedded in the detail of the English landscape, against the painting of a slag heap by

William Scott, or David Hepher's large painting of 1970s social housing blocks. And through the whole group, Perry threads strands of a critical British documentary photography tradition. In the years following the Second World War, and up to the 1980s, great photo-journalists such as Thurston Hopkins, Ian Berry and Martin Parr travelled the country recording daily life in anthropological detail. Often wry and affectionate, sometimes shocking, their photographs reveal other truths about us as a nation, and make an important contribution to this thematically dense exhibition.

We owe a debt of gratitude to Grayson Perry for the intelligence, subtlety and wit that he has brought in equal measure to this project, and for the seriousness with which he has grasped the proposition of drawing an exhibition from the Arts Council Collection. Over many hours of conversation, and looking at work, he has honed a visual argument about a very personal notion of Englishness that bravely skirts stereotypes, and reaches towards something more difficult, and more true to history. The England evoked by *Unpopular Culture* is not all 'long days in the sun, slim volumes of verse', but it is not all grim 'kitchen sink', nor swinging Sixties either; the exhibition is not autobiographical, but yet touches on ideas clearly very rooted in Perry's personal history. The story it tells is not a facile narrative of easily digestible themes, but an attempt to get away from these, and back to the emotional texture of a period that still significantly informs our sense of identity.

I should also like to express our thanks to Blake Morrison, who has written so perceptively about both the art and the poetry that Grayson has chosen to accompany the exhibition, linking themes of nostalgia for a pre-war world of innocence with the optimism of a new socially mobile world after 1945.

The exhibition was originally conceived by Natalie Rudd, Sculpture Curator, based at the Collection's centre in Yorkshire, and has been expertly and elegantly put together by her and Jill Constantine, Senior Curator of the Collection, with unstinting assistance from Lizzie Docherty, Rachel Arndt, Sussanah Chan, Andy Craig and Jonny Aldous, all of whose contribution cannot be underestimated. We are also grateful to Chris McCabe of the Saison Poetry Library at the Royal Festival Hall for his invaluable guidance in suggesting poetry for the catalogue, as well as to colleagues in Hayward Publishing and Touring for their contributions. And last but not least, our thanks to everyone at Victoria Miro for their support of this new and exciting exhibition, which we hope will prove provocative and stimulating to audiences as it tours throughout the UK.

Caroline Douglas
HEAD OF ARTS COUNCIL COLLECTION

Unpopular Culture

Grayson Perry

I HARDLY EVER go to Tate Modern; it has become too popular for me. I can't see the art for backpacks and buggies. It is always full of snapping tourists, screaming school parties and families visiting London for the day. In the Noughties, contemporary art, or at least going to contemporary art galleries, has attained mass appeal. The latest art is often sensational, big, loud, shocking, funny. It is a thrill ride for the people, literally in the case of Carsten Höller's helter-skelters in Tate Modern's Turbine Hall. But I look back to only a quarter of a century ago, when I left art college, and I see contemporary art was a grim, socialist rather than popular, business. Being an artist seemed to be about residencies in coalmines and knitting pro-abortion banners. Being involved with contemporary art felt like living in an inbred backwater rarely visited by the average citizen or the mainstream media. When they did take notice, it was only to confirm outdated prejudices and snigger at the freak show where sculptures were full of holes and a pile of bricks cost as much as a luxury car.

So when the Arts Council Collection asked me to select a touring exhibition of works from their holdings, I had the shrill voice of twenty-first century contemporary art ringing in my ears as it clamoured for attention in our crowded cultural landscape. I was also aware of the remnants of hostility to fine art from *Daily Mail* Britain who still see art as an elitist con. As I trawled through the Arts Council Collection catalogues, illustrating around 7,500 pieces, I found myself drawn to art from the earlier part of the Collection; works that could be characterised as subtle, sensitive, lyrical and quiet. My choices fell into three distinct categories: figurative painting, bronze sculpture and documentary photography. What bound these three groups of work together were the period of their inception – on the whole the works date from 1940 until about 1980 – and also a more ineffable sense of mood. A lack of intellectual audacity and visual showmanship may have excluded some of these artists from the headlines of art history, but for me as a group these artists speak eloquently of Britain in a time between the trauma of the Second World War and the onset of Thatcherite selfish capitalism, a time between the Blitz and the contemporary bombardment by media and marketing. I may be reactionary or nostalgic, but for me these artworks conjure up an age before our experience of ourselves was muffled completely by the commercial and sophisticated intermediaries of television, advertising and digital communications.

My title for the exhibition, *Unpopular Culture*, stems from a notion that, unlike today, in Britain during the period represented by this show, stories about art did not feature daily in the broadsheets nor

8

W.5724.

did contemporary artists crop up frequently in gossip columns. If you had asked a taxi driver in the 1950s to name a British artist, they would probably have struggled to name one. If they could have, it would most likely have been John Bratby, who lived his life in public and vigorously pursued publicity. Artists like Henry Moore and Barbara Hepworth were becoming well known on an international stage. On the whole though, it was a time when modern art did not attract the masses and was seen as an even more rarefied activity, practised and appreciated by other-worldly bohemians and intellectuals. Falling in the middle of this period, British Pop Art did enjoy a flurry of fame but I have not included any work by artists such as Peter Blake, David Hockney or Richard Hamilton. This is partly due to a suspicion that the swinging Sixties, in all its groovy glory, was really only enjoyed by a minority, and partly because I'm a bit tired of the hackneyed nostalgia for a psychedelic, World Cup-winning, Mini-driving, miniskirt-wearing, Beatles-loving supposed golden age. Perhaps I'm guilty of autobiography as analysis, but I was born in 1960 and I am sure I am not the only one for whom the Fab Four were but distant black-and-white spectres on Top of the Pops. In an article in *The Guardian*, Liz Jobey describes photographer Tony Ray-Jones' return to Britain after five years in the United States in 1966 to find London swinging but the rest of Britain still clearly divided by class and tradition. In the decade of cultural revolution, I never went into an

Sculpture in the Home,
1st exhibition, Laing Art
Gallery, Newcastle, 1947

art gallery and didn't even know that homosexuality or recreational drugs existed.

To me, the 1960s blend with the preceding decade, a period that I see in clichéd terms of austerity and anxiety. In 1950, Cyril Connolly in his closing editorial of the magazine *Horizon* famously summed-up the gloomy intimations of mortality in the national post-war psyche when he said, 'From now on an artist will be judged only by the resonance of his solitude and the quality of his despair.' He was thinking of that poster boy of gruesome angst, Francis Bacon. This nuclear age disquiet was famously described by Herbert Read in the catalogue for the British Pavilion at the 1952 Venice Biennale, which featured sculpture by Lynn Chadwick and Kenneth Armitage: 'Images of flight, of ragged claws "scuttling across the floors of silent seas" of excoriated flesh, frustrated sex, the geometry of fear.'

Looking at the works in *Unpopular Culture*, thinking of the past, I feel ambivalent. In the photographs and paintings there is a strand of urban proletarian subject matter, the working class at play. Alan Lowndes, L.S. Lowry, David Hepher, William Roberts, Tony Ray-Jones and Patrick Ward show us glimpses of a lost world of close-knit communities but also gritty domestic horrors. I see littered in the compositions my own memories of fêtes, jolly singsongs and days out in Southend, but also in the worried, weathered faces I recall poverty and intolerance. Their poignancy for me tempered perhaps by a feeling of voyeurism towards the working classes, an uncomfortable remnant of my own class travelling and abandonment of my roots.

There is, I think, a uniquely British thread of hushed romanticism in the paintings of Elinor Bellingham Smith, Paul Nash, Victor Pasmore, John Piper, Alan Reynolds and Leonard Rosoman. They know how to make a virtue of grey as only a Briton can. I find, in these pictures, an attractive humility and elegance, qualities that might be described today as not being media friendly, but which I wish to celebrate.

No matter how hard I try to supplant the thought, the principle association the sculptures I have selected bring to my mind is with childhood trips to concrete New Towns and their architecture of catastrophic optimism. Each bronze is to me an evocation of a guano-spattered plinth on a windswept shopping centre. It was modern art in a public place with no agenda of regeneration. A lot of the Modernist architecture of the 1950s and 1960s now seems quaint compared to the behemoths of Brutalism and Post-Modernism that were to follow, and in the same way I now enjoy these sculptures of the period for their poetry, tradition and restraint compared to the noisy free-for-all that was to come. They are solid and soulful in a way that deserves our fond appreciation, just as grandee art historian Kenneth Clark demonstrates when he spontaneously pats the head of a Henry Moore maquette as he crosses his study in his landmark series of television programmes, *Civilisation*.

The paintings and sculptures that I have selected for *Unpopular Culture* are nearly all figurative. This is a purely personal bias. Abstract art reminds me too much of beardy art lecturers with grey chest hair poking out of their denim shirts as they spout vague unchallenge-able tosh. I associate abstraction with unreconstructed machismo. This prompts me to say that I am sorry there are not more women artists in this show, but the gender imbalance is representative of the holdings of the Collection, which in turn probably reflect the art world of the time.

I have made two works in reply to my selections. They are responses of mood but both refer to one or more specific works. The pot *Queen's Bitter* (2007, cat. 50) picks up on the colours of Jack Smith's *After the Meal* (1952, cat. 70), the painting that I feel is central to the tone of this exhibition. My main influences, though, were the photographs, especially the ethnographic studies of Britain by Tony Ray-Jones and Patrick Ward. These remind me of a more innocent Britain of clubs and hobbies, of 'Knees up Mother Brown' and Mackeson stout. I think of *Queen's Bitter* as a kind of apprentice piece dedicated to beery Britain in the second Elizabethan age. The second piece, *Head of a Fallen Giant* (2007–08, cat. 51), formally relates to the sculptures of William Turnbull and Eduardo Paolozzi via Damien Hirst. It is a large, war-like bronze skull; its subject is the changing face of Britain in the second half of the twentieth century. Perhaps because of multiculturalism, there has been much debate in the media in the last few years about what Britishness is. Some of the artists in this show, such as John Piper, had a great passion for our national heritage. The work of others, such as Frank Auerbach, Paul Nash or Bryan Wynter, is emotionally linked to specific British places – Camden, Dymchurch and Cornwall – and I can think of no more British an eye than that of Martin Parr. In response, I offer an ethnographic artefact, a voodoo relic of a once huge empire encrusted with a boiled-down essence of itself in the form of tourist tat. Routemasters, the three lions, Beefeaters, Big Ben, Tower Bridge, Bulldogs, all hallowed tribal symbols. Symbols that Brits hold more dear than blinging diamonds, I hope.

I have also designed a headscarf, which will be on sale during the exhibition. The headscarf is for me a symbol of womanhood in the period represented by the works in the show – worn to preserve a shampoo and set from the northern damp until the evening visit to the working-men's club, and also sported by the Queen, out tramping the heather in Balmoral. Now, of course, the headscarf has a whole different set of meanings in modern multi-faith Britain.

Putting this show together has been an enjoyable experience. I have chosen chiefly to please myself, but in so doing I have perhaps betrayed my attitude to trends in society and contemporary art. My choices are as much about today as the period of their making.

Through my selections, I seem to be presenting an exhibition that is defiantly not a quick fix of visual stimulation for an adrenaline addicted consumer. *Unpopular Culture* is perhaps a picture of British culture when life was slower and when, maybe, we were more reflective, more civic and more humane.

Waving Goodbye

Blake Morrison

DO ARTISTS see the world the rest of us see? Or are their works purely self-expression, with no tangible connection to historical reality? These questions might seem crude, the implied distinctions dubious. Clearly Vermeer, for example, captured something of seventeenth-century Dutch life, both the people and their houses. And although Italian Renaissance painters took classical and Christian mythology as their subject, an impression of their own time (clothes, faces, décor) does seep through in their work. Still, we would be unwise to deduce from a comparison of Corot and Courbet with Renoir and Monet that French life became more colourful – literally – over the nineteenth century. And if we want to know what the bombing of Guernica looked like, we are better off studying photos and newsreels than consulting Picasso's famous painting.

Yet the Picasso is no less 'true', and conveys that truth more memorably and with greater emotional force than any newsreel can. As an artist, Picasso wasn't just selectively interpreting history (photographers and film editors do that too), but *painting what wasn't there* – expressing ideas invisible to the naked eye and depicting emotions hidden from the lens. When photographers tamper with historical truth, they are liable to be accused of cheating; they can select, crop, compress and enlarge, but inserting faces that weren't present, or deleting bodies that were, will get them in trouble. Painters aren't placed under the same burden of representation. If the woman in the foreground needs a red hat because the structure and colour scheme demand it, then red it must be, even if the artist's model wore blue or the figure in the photographic image used as raw material isn't wearing a hat at all.

The greater freedom that painters enjoy doesn't mean they are unconcerned with authenticity, however. To think of painting as purely fictive, and photography as purely factual, does a disservice to both art forms. Martin Parr's photograph, *Jubilee Street Party, Elland 1977* (1977, cat. 46), for example, is every bit as imaginative (and aesthetically shaped) as a painting would be. And the postures and expressions of the two women in John Bratby's *Jean and Susan* (1956, cat. 10) – clearly sharing some momentous secret – are no less true to life than any photograph. In their different ways, both Parr and Bratby convey something about British society and character. What they are saying cannot be reduced to a simple message but it is social observation nevertheless. Just as Charles Dickens saw things in Victorian society that other contemporary commentators missed, so the visual artists of our own time offer insights we can't find elsewhere.

If painting and sculpture have as much to say about the real world as photography does, what impression does the exhibition *Unpopular Culture* give of Britain

Sculpture in the Home,
1947

in the years 1940–80? It looks a little grey, cold, wan, sludgy, down-at-heel, not bursting with imperial self-confidence but gently adapting to its reduced circumstances. Several of the human figures that appear are round-shouldered, as though bowed down by a sense of loss or depression. But there are cheerful faces to be found, too, taking refuge in drink, religious worship or familial comforts. The nation appears to be predominantly urban, with cars, concrete, lamp-posts, neon. But the countryside is still there, and its open spaces and wistful colours are quietly cherished, without brash celebration. Traditional entertainments persist – the seaside, the circus, fairs, pubs, fights – and the young are venerated, especially in photographs. It's not an affluent country, nor a fashionable one (there is little sign of the swinging Sixties or the conspicuous consumption of the Thatcher years), but it is decent, public-spirited and doing the best it can. George Orwell would have recognised the place and applauded it.

Philip Larkin would have recognised it too. In one of his finest poems, 'To the Sea', he describes a visit to a seaside resort and marvels that its rituals are so little changed from those he knew as a child 40 years earlier:

Steep beach, blue water, towels, red bathing caps,
The small hushed waves' repeated fresh collapse
Up the warm yellow sand, and further off
A white steamer stuck in the afternoon –
Still going on, all of it, still going on!

Larkin published this poem in 1969, and it is interesting to compare it both with William Robert's 1966 painting of the seaside (cat. 62), which portrays ten busy, interwoven, semi-naked, hulking Leger-like figures, all with their backs to us, and with Tony Ray-Jones' 1967 photograph of Brighton beach (cat. 54), which has a row of buttoned-up pensioners sitting, eating and staring into space. All three works delight in the persistence of humdrum, rarely celebrated leisure activities (or inactivities) at a time when they were thought to be disappearing. There's a sense of wonder (beautifully caught in Larkin's exclamation-mark) that neither two world wars nor all the other upheavals of the twentieth century have destroyed some essential continuities of British life. L.S. Lowry's painting *July, the Seaside* (1943, cat. 33), from a quarter of a century earlier, captures the same blithe spirit – immune to the threat of foreign invasion, our island nation disports itself by the sea.

Larkin is an obvious figure to invoke in the context of *Unpopular Culture*, not just because Grayson Perry clearly knows and likes his poetry but because it expresses the same unobtrusive elegance and nostalgia as the works in the show. Like many of his generation, Larkin saw the First World War and the arrival of Modernism (whether that of Ezra Pound, James Joyce, Pablo Picasso, Igor Stravinsky or Charlie Parker) as a moment of rupture. In his poem 'MCMXIV', he pinpoints that moment to 1914, describing men waiting to volunteer for military service and mourning the world that is about to be lost: 'Never such innocence again.' But for all his proclaimed hostility to foreign marauders and their dangerous experiments, Larkin assimilated a great deal from Modernism, as did most of the artists in this show. And for all his nostalgia, he continued to find pockets of uncorrupted innocence. I can imagine him poring over Homer Sykes' photograph *Whit Wednesday Pinner Fair, Pinner, Middlesex* (1969–75, cat. 72), not only because he enjoyed looking at naked ladies but because quirky customs, time-honoured rites and ancient festivals appealed to him.

Larkin would also have been moved, for different reasons, by George Rodger's photograph of the aftermath of the German air-raid on Coventry in 1940. Larkin had grown up in Coventry and two days after the bombing he returned there as a student from Oxford to make sure his parents were alive. Ruined buildings feature strongly in *Unpopular Culture* but newly-constructed ones are here too: a key feature of Welfare State Britain was the construction of blocks of flats for council tenants whose previous homes had been destroyed by German bombs or were deemed uninhabitable slums. Usually thought to be the exclusive province of architects, buildings make a difficult subject for painters, but Michael Andrews and David Hepher, along with the photographer Christine Pearcey, rise to the challenge. Andrews is the most painterly: his *Flats* (1959, cat. 1) look partly Bauhaus and partly otherworldly, marooned as they are in a green landscape, with the odd black brushstroke hinting at human figures. There are no people at all in the other two works. Hepher's is an oil painting of 1979–81 that aspires to both Abstract Expressionism and Hyperrealism. *Arrangement in Turquoise and Cream* (cat. 22), he calls it, for though it looks like a photograph, what interests him is the use of colour and the formal constraint of a Mondrian-like grid. A garage door in the foreground disrupts the patterned severity to give a sense of scale. Pearcey also includes a low foreground building in her *Untitled* 1973 photograph of a tower block (cat. 49), but for a different effect – the three violins hanging from a ramshackle corrugated-iron shed roof create a whimsical counterpoint to the soulless flats massing behind. All three artists are more interested in the formal possibilities offered by blocks of flats than they are in making social comment. But they do leave a visual record. This is what Britain looked like – still looks like. This is where millions live.

Other paintings in the exhibition have a similar representational impetus. Ruskin Spear's painting, *Hammersmith Broadway* (1950, cat. 71), Frank Auerbach's *Euston Steps – Study* (1980–81, cat. 3) and Bryan Wynter's *Landscape, Zennor* (1948, cat. 79): real places in real time. But painting allows for mystery too, and it's there in Elinor Bellingham Smith's *The Island* (1951, cat. 7). Paul Nash's *Promenade* (1922, cat. 40) shows a severe concrete embankment but its grey and white shades are translucent, and the woman walking along in an ankle-length dress is ethereal. Even the Kitchen-Sink realism of Jack Smith's *After the Meal* (1952, cat. 70) is deceptive: the setting is humble (bare floorboards and minimal furniture) but the crockery and cutlery seem to belong to another period and to a more elevated social class. This gets the viewer wondering about the story and what the painting wants to tell us: why is the door open and what is the expression on the face of the girl in the background?

If the class affiliations of the art in *Unpopular Culture* are sometimes ambivalent, that's not surprising, since the artists came from a range of social backgrounds. The 1950s and 1960s were a period of greatly increased social mobility (more than exists today) and the effects of migration from one class to another were much debated. Larkin and his friends among the Movement poets (notably Kingsley Amis) were snootily derided by an earlier generation of writers for being 'lower-middle class'. They also aroused the hostility of some of their own generation, who accused them of being 'suburban'. To this they replied that – irrespective of their origins – they were describing the reality of the Britain they saw. Carel Weight's painting of a (north London?) suburban back garden in the 1970s makes the same claim. *The World We Live In* (1970-73, cat. 77), he calls it, defying us not to recognise the houses, chimneys, leaves, straggling lawns, even the moustached figure in the foreground.

I suspect that Grayson Perry has called his exhibition *Unpopular Culture* for two reasons. Firstly, he believes that a certain strand of British culture has never been given the attention it deserves, because written off as naff, ephemeral or self-effacing. Secondly, he is nostalgic for an age when artists had not yet become fashion icons. He might himself be a media celebrity, but on the evidence of his choices the art he values is introverted, unglamorous and more interested in exploring byways and backwaters than in parading itself on the global stage. He has said that he was drawn to ceramics because he considered it the underdog among art forms. And that same affection for the underdog is evident here – for art that is wholesome, truthful, textured and unflashy.

Anyone knowing only that Grayson Perry is a contemporary artist might have supposed the show would be full of videos, installations and self-conscious interrogations of 'the meaning of art' (there are none). Someone knowing slightly more about him might have expected transvestism, pottery and images of Essex in the 1970s (there are very few). Instead, he has come up with a show that is muted, modest, wary, even at times slightly dour. A show that includes both the famous and the half-forgotten or relatively unknown. A show that is largely devoted to the period 1940-80 but allows in works from before and after that fit the mood. A show that explores the ways in which art adds to our sense of ourselves individually and as a nation. A show to get us looking and thinking.

Plates

Kenneth Armitage
Figure Lying on its Side
(No.5), 1957
cat. 2

Thurston Hopkins
Untitled, 1947–56
cat. 24

George Rodger
*Basement shelter of a
children's hospital during
a bomber raid*, 1940
cat. 65

London Park in Time of Peace

Vernon Scannell

On the blue breast of August bravely burns
The medallion of the polished sun,
White tourniquets of cloud conceal the wounds
Incurred in wintry battles of attrition.

The children's laughter rises like the bright
And liberated kites; adventures rock
At landing-stages waiting for the right
Adventurer to enter; lovers shock

The tight-lipped woman who, accompanied
By all she knows of love on leather leash,
Walks in the glass enclosure of despair
Towards the fragile certainty of tea.

And the iron soldier on the pompous horse
Stares upward, showing neither fear nor wonder;
The stormcloud, turgid, purple, ripe as plum,
Waits for the raping teeth of burly thunder.

Meg Rutherford
Quartros, 1960
cat. 68

David Hurn
Untitled (Two women),
1971–81
cat. 28

Thurston Hopkins
Morecombe and Wise on
Blackpool Beach, 1953.
1953–56
cat. 25

Bryan Kneale
Iron Pig, 1962
cat. 29

David Hepher
*Arrangement in Turquoise
and Cream*, 1979–81
cat. 22

Margaret Lovell
Bronze Box, 1961
cat. 30

The Figure

Tony Harrison

In each of our Blackpool photos from those years
and, I'll bet, in every family's South Pier snap,
behind the couples with their children on the pier, 's
the same figure standing in frayed suit and cap.

We'd come to plunge regardless in the sea,
ball-shrivellingly chill, but subs all gone,
gorge Mrs Moore's Full Board, now ration-free,
glad when *I-Speak-Your-Weight* showed pounds put on.

The first snap that I have 's from '45.
I've never seen a family group so glad
of its brief freedom, so glad to be alive,
no camera would have caught them looking sad.

He's there, in the same frayed suit, in '51,
that figure in each photo at the back
who sent us all sauntering towards the sun
and the tripod, and the biped draped in black.

Lynn Chadwick
Rad Lad, 1961
cat. 14

Tony Ray-Jones
Brighton Beach 1967, 1967
cat. 54

Paul Nash
Promenade, 1922
cat. 40

Patrick Ward
Untitled, 1969–71
cat. 74

Martin Parr
Jubilee Street Party,
Elland 1977, 1977
cat. 46

MCMXIV

Philip Larkin

Those long uneven lines
Standing as patiently
As if they were stretched outside
The Oval or Villa Park,
The crowns of hats, the sun
On moustached archaic faces
Grinning as if it were all
An August Bank Holiday lark;

And the shut shops, the bleached
Established names on the sunblinds,
The farthings and sovereigns,
And dark-clothed children at play
Called after kings and queens,
The tin advertisements
For cocoa and twist, and the pubs
Wide open all day;

And the countryside not caring:
The place-names all hazed over
With flowering grasses, and fields
Shadowing Domesday lines
Under wheat's restless silence;
The differently-dressed servants
With tiny rooms in huge houses,
The dust behind limousines;

Never such innocence,
Never before or since,
As changed itself to past
Without a word – the men
Leaving the gardens tidy,
The thousands of marriages
Lasting a little while longer:
Never such innocence again.

Thurston Hopkins
Harassed father left to cope
with the family, Liverpool 1955,
1947–56
cat. 26

Edwin Pickett
Head, 1962
cat. 52

Alan Lowndes
Telling the Tale, 1964
cat. 32

Elisabeth Frink
Head, 1959
cat. 16

Ruskin Spear
Hammersmith Broadway, 1950
cat. 71

Bert Hardy
A fight springs up between
dockers waiting for work in
the Pool of London, 1949
cat. 20

Patrick Ward
*Untitled (Pearly King &
Queen, East Ham)*, 1969–71
cat. 75

Dahn the Plug'ole

Anon

A muvver was barfin' 'er biby one night,
The youngest of ten and a tiny young mite,
The muvver was pore and the biby was thin,
Only a skelington covered in skin;
The muvver turned rahnd for the soap orf the rack,
She was but a moment, but when she turned back,
The biby was gorn; and in anguish she cried,
'Oh, where is my biby?' — the Angels replied:
'Your biby 'as fell dahn the plug'ole,
Your biby 'as gorn dahn the plug;
The poor little thing was so skinny and thin,
'E oughter been barfed in a jug;
Your biby is perfectly 'appy,
'E won't need a barf any more,
Your biby 'as fell dahn the plug'ole,
Not lorst, but gorn before!'

Francis Morland
Cork Float Figure, 1961
cat. 35

Tish Murtha
Untitled, 1980–81
From 'Youth Unemployment
in the West End of Newcastle',
1980–81
cat. 36

Alan Reynolds
The Village – Winter, 1952
cat. 60

John Piper
Palace of the Bishop of
Winchester (Design for
mural for Merton Priory
Civic Restaurant), 1942–43
cat. 53

Christine Pearcey
Untitled, 1973
cat. 49

Eduardo Paolozzi
The Frog, 1958
cat. 41

Brian Robb
Townscape, 1959
cat. 61

David Hurn
Untitled, 1971–81
cat. 27

Elisabeth Frink
Assassins No.1, 1963
cat. 17

Homer Sykes
Whit Wednesday Pinner Fair,
Pinner, Middlesex, 1969–75
cat. 72

Tish Murtha
Untitled, 1980–81
From 'Youth Unemployment
in the West End of Newcastle',
1980–81
cat. 37

The Whitsun Weddings

Philip Larkin

That Whitsun, I was late getting away:
    Not till about
One-twenty on the sunlit Saturday
Did my three-quarters-empty train pull out,
All windows down, all cushions hot, all sense
Of being in a hurry gone. We ran
Behind the backs of houses, crossed a street
Of blinding windscreens, smelt the fish-dock; thence
The river's level drifting breadth began,
Where sky and Lincolnshire and water meet.

All afternoon, through the tall heat that slept
    For miles inland,
A slow and stopping curve southwards we kept.
Wide farms went by, short-shadowed cattle, and
Canals with floatings of industrial froth;
A hothouse flashed uniquely: hedges dipped
And rose: and now and then a smell of grass
Displaced the reek of buttoned carriage-cloth
Until the next town, new and nondescript,
Approached with acres of dismantled cars

At first, I didn't notice what a noise
    The weddings made
Each station that we stopped at: sun destroys
The interest of what's happening in the shade,
And down the long cool platforms whoops and skirls
I took for porters larking with the mails,
And went on reading. Once we started, though,
We passed them, grinning and pomaded, girls
In parodies of fashion, heels and veils,
All posed irresolutely, watching us go,

As if out on the end of an event
    Waving goodbye
To something that survived it. Struck, I leant
More promptly out next time, more curiously,
And saw it all again in different terms:
The fathers with broad belts under their suits
And seamy foreheads; mothers loud and fat;
An uncle shouting smut, and then the perms,
The nylon gloves and jewellery-substitutes,
The lemons, mauves, and olive-ochres that

(cont.)

Marked off the girls unreally from the rest.
        Yes, from cafés
And banquet-halls up yards, and bunting-dressed
Coach-party annexes, the wedding-days
Were coming to an end. All down the line
Fresh couples climbed aboard: the rest stood round;
The last confetti and advice were thrown,
And, as we moved, each face seemed to define
Just what it saw departing: children frowned
At something dull; fathers had never known

Success so huge and wholly farcical;
        The women shared
The secret like a happy funeral;
While girls, gripping their handbags tighter, stared
At a religious wounding. Free at last,
And loaded with the sum of all they saw,
We hurried towards London, shuffling gouts of steam.
Now fields were building-plots, and poplars cast
Long shadows over major roads, and for
Some fifty minutes, that in time would seem

Just long enough to settle hats and say
        I nearly died,
A dozen marriages got under way.
They watched the landscape, sitting side by side
– An Odeon went past, a cooling tower,
And someone running up to bowl – and none
Thought of the others they would never meet
Or how their lives would all contain this hour.
I thought of London spread out in the sun,
Its postal districts packed like squares of wheat:

There we were aimed. And as we raced across
        Bright knots of rail
Past standing Pullmans, walls of blackened moss
Came close, and it was nearly done, this frail
Travelling coincidence; and what it held
stood ready to be loosed with all the power
That being changed can give. We slowed again,
And as the tightened brakes took hold, there swelled
A sense of falling, like an arrow-shower
Sent out of sight, somewhere becoming rain.

Barbara Hepworth
Spring, 1966
cat. 23

Anthony Caro
Woman Waking Up, 1956
cat. 13

John Myers
Young Boy, 1975
cat. 39

Frank Auerbach
Euston Steps – Study,
1980–81
cat. 3

John Wragg
Trophy, 1963
cat. 78

Edward Burra
Blasted Oak, 1942
cat. 11

Leonard Rosoman
Gardens on Different Levels,
1955
cat. 67

George Rodger
*A London family bombed out of
their home during the night,
salvage a few personal belongings
on the pavement,* 1940
cat. 63

Duncan Grant
Cow Stalls, 1942
cat. 18

Ian Berry
Untitled, 1973–75
cat. 9

Gerry Badger
Near Dundee, Scotland, 1977,
1977
cat. 4

Carel Weight
The World We Live In,
1970–73
cat. 77

Going, Going

Philip Larkin

I thought it would last my time –
The sense that, beyond the town,
There would always be fields
    and farms,
Where the village louts could climb
Such trees as were not cut down;
I knew there'd be false alarms

In the papers about old streets
And split-level shopping, but some
Have always been left so far;
And when the old part retreats
As the bleak high-risers come
We can always escape in the car.

Things are tougher than we are, just
As earth will always respond
However we mess it about;
Chuck filth in the sea, if you must:
The tides will be clean beyond.
– But what do I feel now? Doubt?

Or age, simply? The crowd
Is young in the MI café;
Their kids are screaming for more –
More houses, more parking allowed,
More caravan sites, more pay.
On the Business Page, a score

Of spectacled grins approve
Some takeover bid that entails
Five per cent profit (and ten
Per cent more in the estuaries): move
Your works to the unspoilt dales
(Grey area grants!) And when

You try to get near the sea
In summer …
          It seems, just now,
To be happening so very fast;
Despite all the land left free
For the first time I feel somehow
That it isn't going to last,

That before I snuff it, the whole
Boiling will be bricked in
Except for the tourist parts –
First slum of Europe: a role
It won't be so hard to win,
With a cast of crooks and tarts.

And that will be England gone,
The shadows, the meadows,
    the lanes,
The guildhalls, the carved choirs.
There'll be books; it will linger on
In galleries; but all that remains
For us will be concrete and tyres.

Most things are never meant.
This won't be, most likely: but greeds
And garbage are too thick-strewn
To be swept up now, or invent
Excuses that make them all needs.
I just think it will happen, soon.

Grayson Perry
Head of a Fallen Giant,
2007–08
cat. 51

Grayson Perry
Queen's Bitter, 2007
cat. 50

George Rodger
The morning after the raid on Coventry,
the dead are recovered from the
shambles of what had been a quiet
residential area in the suburbs, 1940
cat. 66

List of Works

All measurements are in centimetres, height x width x depth. Page references are to illustrations in this book. This list was accurate at the time of publication. There may have been subsequent changes to works in the exhibition.

Unless otherwise stated, all works are from the Arts Council Collection, Southbank Centre, London.

1 (p.68)
Michael Andrews (1928–95)
Flats, 1959
Oil on board
105.4 x 138.4
ACA 1

2 (p.18)
Kenneth Armitage (1916–2002)
Figure Lying on its Side (No.5), 1957
Bronze
38.1 x 82.5 x 22.3
AC 450

3 (p.71)
Frank Auerbach (b.1931)
Euston Steps – Study, 1980–81
Oil on board
122.6 x 152.7
AC 4055

4 (p.81)
Gerry Badger (b.1948)
Near Dundee, Scotland, 1977, 1977
Gelatin silver print, selenium toned
18.7 x 26
ACP 0770

5 (p.74)
Gerry Badger
Essex, 1980, 1980
Gelatin silver print
19.3 x 24.2
ACP 1229

6
Clive Barker (b.1940)
Head of Francis Bacon, 1978
Bronze and brass
18.8 x 13 x 13.8
AC 1931

7 (p.22)
Elinor Bellingham Smith
(1906–88)
The Island, 1951
Oil on canvas
142.2 x 182.9
AC 195

8
John Benton-Harris (b.1939)
*Medieval Lady in Rose Garden,
Greenwich, London, Summer 1979*,
1979
Silver bromide print
32 x 21
ACP 1373

9 (p.79)
Ian Berry (b.1934)
Untitled, 1973–75
Silver bromide print
30.5 x 20.7
ACP 0891
© Ian Berry/Magnum Photos

10 (p.20)
John Bratby (1928–92)
Jean and Susan, 1956
Oil on board
122 x 97.5
AC 416
© John Bratby Estate by courtesy
of Julian Hartnoll

11 (p.73)
Edward Burra (1905–76)
Blasted Oak, 1942
Watercolour on paper
50.1 x 61.6
AC 109

12
Edward Burra
Winter, 1964
Watercolour on cardboard
134.6 x 80
ACC2/1965

13 (p.69)
Anthony Caro (b.1924)
Woman Waking Up, 1956
Bronze
30.5 x 66 x 38
AC 459
© Barford Sculptures Ltd

14 (p.33)
Lynn Chadwick (1914–2003)
Rad Lad, 1961
Bronze
29.2 x 9.5 x 9.5
AC 602

15
Robert Colquhoun (1914–62)
Church Lench, 1942
Oil on canvas
50.8 x 60.5
AC 63

16 (p.45)
Elisabeth Frink (1930–93)
Head, 1959
Bronze
27.3 x 41.3 x 18.4
AC 499
© Frink Estate

17 (p.61)
Elisabeth Frink
Assassins No.1, 1963
Bronze
56 x 17 x 12
AC 797
© Frink Estate

18 (p.78)
Duncan Grant (1885–1978)
Cow Stalls, 1942
Oil on canvas
43 x 53
AC 95
© Estate of Duncan Grant/
Licensed by DACS 2008

19 (p.46)
Bert Hardy (1913–95)
Pub scene in the Gorbals, 1948
Silver bromide print
34 x 44.5
ACP 0211 (ACP 0182)

20 (p.49)
Bert Hardy
*A fight springs up between dockers
waiting for work in the Pool of
London*, 1949
Silver bromide print
24 x 31.6
ACP 0191

21 (p.76)
Anthony Hatwell (b.1931)
*Still life with Jug, Fruit and
Draperies*, 1959
Bronze
26.7 x 40 x 37.5
AC 517

22 (p.30)
David Hepher (b.1935)
*Arrangement in Turquoise and
Cream*, 1979–81
Oil on canvas
193 x 275
AC 5010

23 (p.67)
Barbara Hepworth (1903–75)
Spring, 1966
Paint, string and bronze
76.8 x 50.8 x 38.1
AC 869

24 (p.19)
Thurston Hopkins (b.1913)
Untitled, 1947–56
Silver bromide print
30.7 x 45.5
ACP 0254
© Thurston Hopkins/
Getty Images 2007

25 (p.28)
Thurston Hopkins
*Morecombe and Wise on Blackpool
Beach, 1953*, 1953–56
Silver bromide print
30.7 x 21
ACP 0233
© Thurston Hopkins/
Getty Images 2007

26 (p.41)
Thurston Hopkins
*Harassed father left to cope with
the family, Liverpool 1955*, 1955–56
Silver bromide print
23 x 33
ACP 0258
© Thurston Hopkins/
Getty Images 2007

27 (p.60)
David Hurn (b.1934)
Untitled, 1971–81
Gelatin silver print
37.5 x 25
ACP 1317
© David Hurn/Magnum Photos

28 (p.27)
David Hurn
Untitled (Two women), 1971–81
Gelatin silver print
37.5 x 25
ACP 1320
© David Hurn/Magnum Photos

29 (p.29)
Bryan Kneale (b.1930)
Iron Pig, 1962
Iron
38.1 x 50.8 x 35.6
AC 656

30 (p.31)
Margaret Lovell (b.1939)
Bronze Box, 1961
Bronze
29.8 x 33 x 17.1
AC 604

31
Alan Lowndes (1921–78)
Entering the Circus (1), 1963
Oil on canvas
99 x 81.3
ACA 58

32 (p.44)
Alan Lowndes
Telling the Tale, 1964
Oil on board
54.6 x 81.3
ACA 59

33 (p.48)
L.S. Lowry (1887–1976)
July, the Seaside, 1943
Oil on canvas
66.7 x 92.7
ACC1/1943
© The Estate of LS Lowry

34 (p.62)
Henry Moore (1898–1986)
Seated Figure Against a Curved Wall,
1957
Bronze
56.5 x 91.4 x 53.3
AC 485

35 (p.53)
Francis Morland (b.1934)
Cork Float Figure, 1961
Bronze
59.7 x 15.9 x 19
AC 670

36 (p.54)
Tish Murtha (b.1956)
Untitled, 1980–81
From 'Youth Unemployment in the
West End of Newcastle', 1980–81
Gelatin silver print
26.1 x 39.3
ACP 1461

37 (p.64)
Tish Murtha
Untitled, 1980–81
From 'Youth Unemployment in the
West End of Newcastle', 1980–81
Gelatin silver print
25.8 x 39.3
ACP 1464

38 (p.83)
John Myers (b.1944)
Young Girl, 1972–73
Silver bromide print
17.5 x 23
ACP 0574

39 (p.70)
John Myers
Young Boy, 1975
Silver bromide print
23 x 18
ACP 0582

40 (p.35)
Paul Nash (1889–1946)
Promenade, 1922
Watercolour on paper
36.8 x 69.9
AC 31
© Tate, London 2008

41 (p.58)
Eduardo Paolozzi (1924–2005)
The Frog, 1958
Bronze
68.6 x 81.3 x 86.2
AC 661
© Trustees of the Paolozzi
Foundation, Licensed by
DACS 2008

42
Eduardo Paolozzi
The Old King, c.1963
Bronze
27.9 x 20.3 x 12.1
AC 747

43
Martin Parr (b.1952)
Hebden Bridge, Holywell Green,
1975
Silver bromide print
16.1 x 24.2
ACP 0416

44
Martin Parr
*Hebden Bridge, Steep Lane
Buffet Lunch*, 1977
Silver bromide print
16.1 x 24.2
ACP 0403

45
Martin Parr
Hebden Bridge, Steep Lane Chapel,
1977
Silver bromide print
16.1 x 24.1
ACP 0404

46 (p.38)
Martin Parr
Jubilee Street Party, Elland 1977, 1977
Silver bromide print
16.2 x 24.3
ACP 0417
© Martin Parr/Magnum Photos

47 (p.80)
Victor Pasmore (1908–98)
Riverside Gardens, Hammersmith,
c.1944
Oil on canvas
45.7 x 61
ACC2/1957

48
Christine Pearcey (b.unknown)
Untitled, 1973
Silver bromide print
36.5 x 24.4
ACP 0901

49 (p.57)
Christine Pearcey
Untitled, 1973
Silver bromide print
36.5 x 25
ACP 0906

50 (p.86)
Grayson Perry (b.1960)
Queen's Bitter, 2007
Ceramic
57 x 134
Courtesy the Artist and Victoria
Miro Gallery, London
© The Artist/Victoria Miro
Gallery 2008

51 (p.85)
Grayson Perry
Head of a Fallen Giant, 2007–08
Bronze
38 x 52 x 38
Courtesy the Artist and Victoria
Miro Gallery, London
© The Artist/Victoria Miro
Gallery 2008

52 (p.43)
Edwin Pickett (b.1938)
Head, 1962
Bronze
35.6 x 14 x 15.9
AC 794

53 (p.56)
John Piper (1903–92)
*Palace of the Bishop of Winchester
(Design for mural for Merton Priory
Civic Restaurant)*, 1942–43
Gouache on paper
40.6 x 52
AC 217
© The Piper Estate

54 (p.34)
Tony Ray-Jones (1941–72)
Brighton Beach 1967, 1967
Silver bromide print
17.7 x 26.8
ACP 1086
© National Media Museum/
Science and Society Picture Library

55
Tony Ray-Jones
Beauty Contest, Southport 1968,
1968
Silver bromide print
17.7 x 26.6
ACP 1091

56
Tony Ray-Jones
Blackpool 1968, 1968
Silver bromide print
26.6 x 17.6
ACP 1085

57
Tony Ray-Jones
Blackpool 1968, 1968
Silver bromide print
26.5 x 17.6
ACP 1092

58
Tony Ray-Jones
Coconut Dancers, Bacup 1968,
1968
Silver bromide print
17.4 x 26
ACP 1095

59
Tony Ray-Jones
Durham Miners Gala 1969, 1969
Silver bromide print
26.8 x 17.6
ACP 1089

60 (p.55)
Alan Reynolds (b.1926)
The Village – Winter, 1952
Oil on board
61 x 91.8
AC 247

61 (p.59)
Brian Robb (1913–79)
Townscape, 1959
Oil on canvas
76.8 x 63.8
AC 545

62 (p.36)
William Roberts (1895–1980)
The Seaside, c.1966
Oil on canvas
61 x 76.2
AC 863

63 (p.77)
George Rodger (1908–95)
*A London family bombed out of their
home during the night, salvage a
few personal belongings on the
pavement*, 1940
Silver bromide print
21 x 30.2
ACP 0732
© George Rodger/Magnum
Photos

64
George Rodger
*An East End family in shelter
during raid*, 1940
Silver bromide print
21 x 30.2
ACP 0739

65 (p.21)
George Rodger
*Basement shelter of a children's
hospital during a bomber raid*, 1940
Silver bromide print
21 x 30.2
ACP 0740
© George Rodger/Magnum
Photos

66 (p.87)
George Rodger
*The morning after the raid on
Coventry, the dead are recovered
from the shambles of what had
been a quiet residential area in
the suburbs*, 1940
Silver bromide print
20.7 x 30
ACP 0735
© George Rodger/Magnum
Photos

67 (p.75)
Leonard Rosoman (b.1913)
Gardens on Different Levels, 1955
Oil on canvas
62 x 75
AC 377

68 (p.25)
Meg Rutherford (1932–2006)
Quartros, 1960
Bronze
8.3 x 33 x 20.3
AC 571

69 (p.42)
William Scott (1913–89)
Slagheap Landscape, 1953
Oil on canvas
71 × 91
ACC5/1953
© William Scott Foundation 2008

70 (p.26)
Jack Smith (b.1928)
After the Meal, 1952
Oil on canvas
112 × 121
AC 260

71 (p.47)
Ruskin Spear (1911–90)
Hammersmith Broadway, 1950
Oil on board
45 × 34
AC 183

72 (p.63)
Homer Sykes (b.1949)
*Whit Wednesday Pinner Fair,
Pinner, Middlesex*, 1969–75
Silver bromide print
33 × 22.2
ACP 1625
© the artist 2008
www.homersykes.com

73 (p.40)
William Turnbull (b.1922)
Head, 1955
Bronze
22.9 × 22.9 × 61
AC 544

74 (p.37)
Patrick Ward (b.1937)
Untitled, 1969–71
Silver bromide print
20.5 × 30.5
ACP 0656
© photograph by Patrick Ward

75 (p.50)
Patrick Ward
*Untitled (Pearly King & Queen,
East Ham)*, 1969–71
Silver bromide print
30.5 × 20.5
ACP 0663
© photograph by Patrick Ward

76 (p.52)
Patrick Ward
Untitled, 1974
Silver bromide print
15.5 × 23
ACP 0665
© photograph by Patrick Ward

77 (p.82)
Carel Weight (1908–97)
The World We Live In, 1970–73
Oil on board
120.5 × 94.5
AC 1549
© the artist 1973

78 (p.72)
John Wragg (b.1937)
Trophy, 1963
Aluminium
91.4 × 35.6 × 25.4
AC 716

79 (p.24)
Bryan Wynter (1915–75)
Landscape, Zennor, 1948
Gouache on canvas
48.3 × 73.7
AC 49
© DACS 2008